NO
JUMP
in my
TRUNK

AN INSPIRING LESSON ON UNPACKING
YOUR POWER AND GETTING A LIFE

NO JUMP
in my
TRUNK

An Inspiring Lesson on Unpacking
Your Power and Getting a Life

By

Chrissie Dixon

REDHAWK
PUBLICATIONS

No Jump in My Trunk

Copyright © 2024 Crystal Dula Dixon

ISBN: 978-1-959346-77-7 (Paperback)

Library of Congress Control Number: 2024947779

Any references to historical events, real people, or places are fictitious. Names, characters, and places are products of the author's imagination.

Book Cover: Ben Precup

Book Layout: Erin Mann

Printed in the United States of America.

First printing edition 2024

Redhawk Publications

The Catawba Valley Community College Press

2550 Hwy 70 SE

Hickory NC 286021

https://redhawkpublications.com

SCAN ME

This story is dedicated to my mother,
who always recognized, appreciated, and
nurtured her children's unique
and individual strengths.

TABLE OF CONTENTS

"There is more in us than we know if we can be made to see it, perhaps for the rest of our lives we will be unwilling to settle for less."

Kurt Haun - Founder of Outward Bound.

Stir up the gift of God which is in you.

2 Timothy 1:6

Be yourself. Everyone else is already taken.

Oscar Wilde

FOREWORD

No Jump in My Trunk is an engaging parable that unveils how rooted origins of self-doubt, when left unchecked, can hinder growth in our lives and careers.

This story is about a family of elephants who daily seek out their own happiness until one of them is sent out into the world only to find that she lacks jump. "Jump" being a metaphor for whatever you do not possess yet strongly believe that you need to be successful in life.

Jump can be many things including education, physical appearance, natural abilities, money, relationships, careers, or social acceptance. The moral tale woven into this short read offers a lesson in taking courage to own and leverage your unique strengths.

The main character, Ella, copes with an abrupt change, imposter syndrome, and the sudden awareness of lacking Jump, before finding her true leader within.

When you embrace the saying "an elephant's gift makes way for her," you will understand the importance of celebrating the talent of others while finding the courage to use your power to maneuver through daily challenges toward a more successful future.

The Cast of Characters

The Herd – A social group of elephants, typically led by a matriarch and consisting of related females and their offspring ranging in size from a small group of around 5-10 to large groups of up to 50 or more. The herd is a metaphor for the organization, team, network, or social circle of people you connect, engage, and associate with in your professional or personal life.

Furaha (pronounced foo-**RAH**-ha) – Swahili for "joy or happiness." A positive state of well-being, contentment, and fulfillment.

Malika (pronounced muh-**LEE**-kah) – Swahili for "leader." She is the herd's matriarch, representing family and close relationships in your personal or professional life that nurture and support you.

Ada (pronounced **AH**-dah) – Swahili for "first daughter." She is inherently next in line for Matriarch and represents people we identify as privileged in our fields of study or activities that generate feelings of resentment or frustration, especially when these individuals are seen as having attained success more easily or with less effort than others have had to apply.
Privilege can manifest in various ways in both our personal and career realms. Economic status, family support and genetic health are some examples.

Mosi (pronounced **MOH**-see) – Swahili for "first son." Born a male elephant, he is not expected to stay with the female herd after adolescence. This character represents individuals that we see as naturally gifted in our fields of study or interests creating feelings of envy or inadequacy, when our hard work isn't yielding similar results. Inherent talents can emerge in diverse ways across various careers and activities, whether through intellectual, athletic, or creative abilities.

Ella (pronounced Ehl-lah) – The middle child heroine that represents all of us who have ever believed a lie about ourselves, doubted our abilities, or undervalued our power.

The Great Egret (pronounced ee-gruht) – A symbol of wisdom, truth, and honesty in African folklore. Here she represents "social and cultural hierarchies" implying that certain talents, abilities, or skills are more valuable or important than others. This system of thinking leads to a narrow definition of worth and success limiting potential and diverse contributions and is propagated through society by media, culture, education, and social norms.

The Lie – Unresolved issues, past traumas or negative experiences that resurface when faced with new challenges.

A Fixed Mindset – Coined by Stanford psychologist Carol Dweck, it is the belief that personal abilities, talents, and intelligence are innate and cannot be changed or developed. This mindset avoids challenges, ignores feedback, and is threatened by others' success.

Stay-Putter – In draw poker, the term "stay putter" typically refers to a player who does not draw any new cards to improve their hand, deciding instead to keep their original hand in hopes of winning without improvement. Much the same, in this story a stay putter is someone who has allowed certain words, actions, or implications to foster a fixed mindset leaving them feeling anxious and defeated when faced with challenges.

Mantra – A focused word or phrase that is repeated in the mind. Typically positive, it is intended to promote focus and personal growth however negative repetitive self-talk can have detrimental effects.

Your Power – A combination of your personality, T.A.G.S (Talents, Abilities, Gifts, and Skills.) and valuable lessons you've learned along the way.

Camp Get A Life – Symbolizes change. Showing how our goals, situations, or conditions in life can shift unexpectedly, often beyond our control. Providing an opportunity to mobilize all available resources- physical, emotional, psychological and social creating a support system that enables us to navigate change more effectively.

Leader Llama – The camp facilitator representing people that you encounter or meet along the road of life who offer encouragement and good counsel.

The Four Campers: Together, they represent the four classic personality temperaments commonly referred to as choleric, phlegmatic, melancholic, and sanguine.

Chi (pronounced chee) - driven/ controlling - she jumps ahead

Golee (pronounced **GO**-lee) –calm/ indecisive - she jumps behind

Tria (pronounced **TREE**-uh) - creative/critical - she jumps in

Otera (pronounced **OH**-te-rah) - enthusiastic/ impulsive - she jumps out

A Growth Mindset – A concept introduced by Stanford psychologist Carol Dweck, that personal abilities, talents, and intelligence can be developed and expanded through effort, persistence, and embracing challenges. This mindset demonstrates tenacity, values feedback, and supports the success of others.

JUMP – A metaphor for an innate ability or specific entitlement you do not possess yet strongly believe that you need to be successful in life.

As you turn the page, please allow the story of *No JUMP in My Trunk* to ignite your imagination leading you to greater self-awareness and embracement of your own talents' abilities, gifts, and skills.

I hope that in doing so, you will nurture a genuine appreciation for the capabilities of those around you, cultivate a more positive and supportive environment, thrive, collaborate, and, most importantly, find your true Joy.

THE PARABLE OF
NO JUMP IN MY TRUNK

THE HERD

There once was a family of Elephants who were members of a tightly bonded herd in the African Savannah where they lived their lives pursuing and finding their daily dose of furaha. The mother was named Malika and she had three children. Ada was the eldest daughter, followed by Ella, the middle child, with Mosi as the youngest and only son.

They were a happy family with many common interests and similarities, though each one possessed desires, abilities, and characteristics that led them to seek out their own special furaha. The family went about their daily routines instinctively, gravitating toward interests that activated their unique types of Joy.

The mother held the esteemed title of Matriarch and had the enormous responsibility of caring and providing for the herd. She accepted this honor with pleasure, allowing it to fill her busy days with furaha.

Ada's birthright entitled her to follow in her mother's footsteps and this great expectation stimulated her mind with continuous thoughts of furaha.

Mosi, who was naturally built for adventure, triggered his furaha through exploration and physical and mental challenges.

Then there was Ella who rose early each morning smiling and happy, spending her days encouraging and motivating all the members of the herd to seek furaha for themselves. Ella did not recognize her gift of exhortation, nor did she understand the power of promoting furaha within the herd. She only knew that in doing so she increased her own.

Mother Elephant took immense pride in all her children's talents, trusting that an elephant's gift makes room for her.

One day, Ella was out trumpeting good morning greetings to everyone she met when she stopped short, hearing hushed tones in the brush. "It's true and everyone knows it," said the great egret sitting atop an old elephant cow. "The sister Ada is incredibly beautiful," the egret continued, "and her good fortune gained by birth is a gift to the herd as our next queen. Then there is the young bull, Mosi. He is strong and brave with a natural drive to explore, and it will not be long before his instincts pull him away from the herd for a life of great adventure. But," she leaned forward, lowering her voice causing her eager audience to strain to hear. "Like I was saying, that middle one, Ella," she added a dramatic pause, "she is a positive and creative child but a stay-putter if ever there was one. Dare I say, there is nothing special about Ella, but at least she can always be counted on to support the herd."

The egret congregation nodded in loyal agreement. "After all," she added, stretching her long neck with self-appointed authority, "stay-putters are essential to the herd."

Ella recoiled at hearing the words. "Not special," echoed over and over as she raced back to the safety of her family. She decided it was best not to mention what she had heard, but even so, it did not take long before the predictions started coming true.

It began with Ada, who became inseparable from their mother, shadowing her every move in preparation for her future role. Mosi started socializing more with the other young males and spending less and less time with the herd. Simultaneously, her mom, with a display of enthusiasm, took Ella aside and explained that she was now mature enough to be trusted with additional responsibilities.

Ella stared blankly as her mom laid it all out.

"I was thinking that you could spend more time helping with the calves. You are patient and understanding," her mother said as she continued to highlight all of Ella's good qualities.

But Ella was not listening; she just nodded, surrendering to her fate. After that, each day became just like the next for Ella. She no longer woke with furaha, nor did she search for it within the herd. Instead, she developed a task-oriented schedule, and by the end of the dry season felt validated by her routine. When herd members shared innovative ideas, she pushed back with "That's not the way this herd does it." And Ella's face adopted a sullen look whenever conversations turned to others' adventures or accomplishments. This sense of control nurtured Ella's fixed mindset. Believing that her qualities were unchanging, she overlooked feedback and evaded challenges as she ruminated daily on the fact that she was a not-special stay-putter, driven by the false security that at least she was essential.

Life Happens

One morning just after the karoo thrush had begun its song, Ella was nudged awake by her mother. The matriarch gestured for her to follow, and Ella immediately obeyed, curious to find out what was going on. The matriarch walked with a wrinkled brow searching for the right words. She had noticed a change in her daughter and wanted very much to help put her back on her path to furaha.

"Do you remember the time," she said aloud, disturbing the silence. "When you motivated the herd to alter our route, saving us from an encounter with a swarm of bees?"

Ella felt the hair rise on her back at the mere mention of this memory. Although she had never been stung, she harbored a terror of bees and had developed the ability to detect their sound from a mile away. On that day she had been first to hear the slight hum of their wings and wasted no time in communicating the need to divert course. Despite her age, Ella had been able to persuade the others to head in a safer direction.

Blushing, Ella recalled the rush of furaha she had felt after the fear had passed.

"I was very proud of you that day, Ella," her mother said, now looking directly at her.

Ella returned her gaze, focusing on her mom's growing smile. "I have good news young lady", the matriarch announced. "You have been selected to represent our herd at this year's Camp Get A Life."

An elephant's gift makes
room for her.

No JUMP in my Trunk

"Wh-what?!" Ella stammered, her eyes rapidly blinking.

Camp Get A Life is an outdoor adventure retreat that inspires animals from all walks of life to use their abilities to discover Furaha beyond their self-perceived limitations.

"Me attend GAL Camp?" Ella said, "But how?"

"You were selected," came her mother's reply.

"When?" Ella's voice cracked.

"Tomorrow," her mother said.

"Why me?" Ella asked.

"Why not you?" Malika moved in closer to her daughter, eyebrows raised with concern.

"This must be a joke," Ella said, forcing a laugh that did not sound very convincing. "I mean, I can't. I insist that you choose someone else."

"You insist?" Malika's tone sharpened.

Ella squeezed her eyes shut and with her pulse in her throat, Ella struggled to speak calmly. "Mom, please, I am not cut out for this. What about Ada? She is the obvious choice as the gift to the herd. Shouldn't she be the one to go?"

Her mother looked surprised. "Gift to the herd?" she repeated. "Where did that come from?"

But Ella kept talking, her words growing more desperate as this new reality was sinking in…. "Or..or..send brother,"

She who does not know one
thing knows another.

African Proverb

she suggested, grasping for straws. "He is the brave adventurer. I bet he would just love a crack at it."

"Honey," Malika said, wrapping her trunk lovingly around Ella's slumped body. "Please tell me where you picked up those exaggerated descriptions of your siblings."

"It doesn't matter where, Mom," Ella said, refusing to meet her eyes. "All that matters is they were right." Tears were swelling in her eyes and running down her trunk. "The simple truth is that I'm not a chosen leader with a destiny or blessed with natural abilities. I'm just me, a stay-putter." Ella gasped, saying the phrase out loud for the first time. "I'm not special Ella," she added, before dissolving into tears.

"My dear, sweet Ella," her mother said, stroking her head and back. "Proverbs say that she who does not know one thing knows another." She was finally beginning to understand the reason behind her daughter's withdrawal from her pursuit of furaha. "Hmm," she said, choosing her words wisely. "So, this is the mantra you have been playing in your head."

"Mantra?" asked Ella, sniffing back tears. "What's a mantra?"

"A mantra is a word or phrase concentrated on and repeated frequently in the mind," said the matriarch. "And yours, my dear, is not a positive one." Ella was offering another excuse when her mother reached out, lifting her chin. "The selection is final; you have been chosen. I don't know to whom you've been listening." She was staring down at Ella with an unwavering eye. "But proverbs say that gossiping and lying go hand in hand. So, decide now

Gossiping and lying go hand in hand.

African Proverb

if you will try to be successful at camp life or continue allowing a lie to make you afraid, closed-minded, and staying put."

Taking a cleansing breath, Ella whispered her response. "But even if I wanted to attend camp, how can I?"

"Well," her mother said," relaxing her eyes. "If you choose to go to camp, I promise that you will have everything you need to be successful in your trunk."

Ella took a hard swallow, and then, believing more in her mother's promise than in herself, responded with, "Okay, I'll just do it."

"Good," said her mother, admiring Ella's fortitude. "Next step, cheer up and unpack your power."

"Cheer up?" Ella's face wrinkled.

"Yes," her mom laughed. "Cheer up means to take heart or take courage. It is the first step in every monumental life change."

"What about unpacking my power?" Ella asked. "I don't think I have any." Mother Elephant raised one eyebrow and quoted, "Proverbs say if you think you are too small to make a difference, you haven't spent a night with a mosquito." Now they were both laughing.

"But seriously Ella," the matriarch continued, "your power is a combination of your personality, talents, abilities, gifts, and skills plus valuable lessons gathered along the way."

If you think you are too small to
make a difference, you haven't
spent a night with a mosquito.

African Proverb

Ella repeated the instructions. "Cheer up and just unpack my power."

"Hey, that's it." Her mom flapped her ears. "That's your new mantra. "Cheer up and just unpack my power." She gave Ella a tight squeeze. "You keep repeating that and I'll get your things ready for camp."

The morning air was cool as they headed toward base camp.

"Why so early?" Ella interrupted her question with a yawn while tying the trunk her mom had packed around her waist in fanny-pack fashion.

"Proverbs say, rising early makes the road short," Ella's mom said with a loving glance back at the resting elephant figures still cloaked in darkness.

"Well, I hope you are right about me having everything I need in this trunk," Ella said struggling to carry her luggage and match her mother's confident stride.

"Hope never fails," replied Malika with peaceful wisdom.

Ella rolled her eyes. Her mom was always quoting proverbs. Easy for her to talk about unpacking power, Ella sighed. Her presence was the essence of power. Everything Queen Malika said and did was powerful, and watching her peripherally, Ella wondered how she could have any idea what it felt like to be afraid and not special.

Hope never fails.

Mother Elephant

"You know Ella," her mom commented as if reading her mind. "Proverbs also say that there are no shortcuts to the top of the palm tree."

"Geesh," Ella thought, but replied instead with "Yes, ma'am" quickening her pace to keep up for the long walk ahead.

"We have arrived!" Malika announced at last. And there it was, Camp Get A Life. Ella stood leg-locked taking in the curious sight she saw around her. It was unlike anything she had ever seen. All kinds of animals in all sorts of shapes and sizes were walking about, talking, laughing, and doing activities. Some were alone, some were in pairs, and others in groups. They were racing, carrying canoes, playing hacky sack, filling up canteens, and passing out sleeping bags.

Ella's eye caught a young cheetah doing pull-ups on a nearby branch. A dog covered in tattoos and other animals were cheering and counting each chin raise. She had never seen so many varied species associating together at the same time unless she counted the water hole during the dry season, and that in no way compared to this.

Searching for the right words, Ella turned to her mom, but the matriarch was not there. Spinning around she caught a glimpse of her as she neared the forest edge.

Turning, the wise matriarch rumbled lovingly, communicating a seismic vibration to Ella. "Remember your mantra," she said.

There are no shortcuts to the top of the palm tree.

African Proverb

"Cheer up and just unpack my power." Then she slipped into the forest.

"Ella!" Ella fanned her ears instinctively, "Momma?" "Ella!" There it was again. It was her name all right, but it was not her mom's voice. "Is there an Ella here?"

"Yes, I am here," Ella said, turning around and running toward a reddish long-necked llama, who was wildly waving a paper in her direction while insisting on bleating her name loudly through a megaphone.

"I'm here, I'm Ella!"

The llama smiled revealing a split lip. Ella was taken aback.

"Welcome Ella, I'm Leader Llama and I will be your cruise director for the next couple of days." She laughed at her own joke displaying two, or was it three sharp pairs of bottom teeth,

Ella smiled politely trying not to stare. "Pleased to meet you," she said, hardly recognizing her own voice.

Leader Llama checked off Ella's name and then motioned for the animals around the tree to join them. "Now that we are all present and accounted for, we can get started," she said.

FAKE QUAKE

Surveying the group Leader Llama nodded her head in satisfaction. "OK, let's see if I can get this right. Take a good look at each other," she said, waiting for the five participants to do so.

Ella glanced around timidly, questioning what she was doing there.

"For the next two days, you will consider the rest of us as your herd, colony, coalition, romp, and pack." The llama smiled with pride after naming each camper's collective noun.

Ella knew then that she was going to be seeing a lot of those teeth.

"Young ladies, please know that Camp Get A Life is a chance to stir up your gifts and awaken the leader inside of you. It offers a safe environment to find out not only who you are but to discover what more there is and refuse to settle for less. This adventure will stretch your limitations and push you out of your comfort zone. You will be tested, and you will have both victories and defeats, but each of you should find confidence in knowing that you were hand-selected because of the potential you already possess, and my desire as your guide is that by the end of our time together you will have a better understanding and appreciation for your abilities and will leave here confident in knowing that you possess within you all that is needed to obtain true furaha in your lives."

After this heartfelt speech, the llama began going through a handout listing the dos and don'ts of the course.

Ella used the opportunity to take another glance at the other campers standing around with their packs and trunks. Each of them looked more confident and capable than she did. Tiny beads of sweat broke out on her forehead and neck. She felt like a fraud. Her heart pounded with the realization that she was only chosen because her mother was the matriarch. Would they see that she did not belong here? Or worse, did they already know? "Any questions?" Ella tuned back into the briefing.

"Yes," replied an animal with webbed hind feet and a long round tail, before clearing her throat. "It says here on page one, paragraph two, only pack what you can use. Please elaborate."

"I'm glad you asked," said Leader Llama. "We will do a lot of walking on this course, so I suggest you do not weigh yourself down with needless items. I am not just speaking of physical stuff but also useless mental baggage."

"Camp Get A Life is a great time to start cleaning your mind of negative thinking and if you decide to leave your bags at this location, our logistical staff will take them downriver for you to collect before we separate into our campsites for the reflective solo portion of the course."

Ella and three others placed their items on a nearby tarp, but the cautious rodent surveyed the scene and decided to pass on the offer.

"To get us started, I'd like to warm up with an icebreaker that will help us get to know each other better," the llama said, quickly

rounding everyone into a small circle. "The rules are simple. Everyone will tell us three things about themselves. Two true things and one false thing. The rest of us will try to guess which thing isn't true."

"Sounds fun," said the energetic otter, stepping toward the middle of the circle before Leader Llama could finish speaking. "Sure does," said the confident cheetah, "I'll go first." She pushed past the otter who showed a flicker of annoyance before her friendly demeanor returned.

"My name is Chi, spelled with an i," the cheetah said, standing with her paws on her hips, feet spread apart as if she was giving everyone time to soak in her awesomeness. Ella was totally soaking it in.

"Number one, I thrive on competition," Chi said. Crossing her arms and drawing herself up to her full height. It seemed to Ella that Chi was looking directly at her. "Number two, I am undemanding, and number three, I will jump ahead and lead the way to victory."

The otter clapped her hands in approval.

"I know the untruth," the dog said in admiration. "It's the second one, the undemanding part."

"You can count on it," Chi said, before returning to her spot in the circle.

"Thanks for getting us started, Chi," the llama said. "That

was a very, shall we say, direct start to this non-confrontational initiative." However, Ella was stuck on something Chi had said. Jump ahead. Jump? The word was unfamiliar to her. She decided to shrug it off as some kind of cheetah thing.

"My turn," said the enthusiastic otter, reporting to the middle for a second time still clapping for Chi, Ella assumed, or possibly just clapping to… just be clapping.

"Good morning, everyone," she projected her voice. "I am Otera, and I'm very excited to be on this amazing life adventure with you."

Ella was unsure why, but now she too felt like clapping.

"To start, I'm reserved. Next, I'm optimistic. And lastly, I'm looking forward to jumping out to make this the best GAL camp ever!" She gave a slight nod as she said each of the last three words, GAL-Camp-Ever.

"No mystery there," said the web-footed rodent without looking up, totally immersed in the task of reorganizing her backpack. "Your untruth is obviously that you are reserved."

"You guessed it!" said Otera. Then chanted "good job, good job, good job" in the direction of the preoccupied student, who still did not look up.

"Jumping out," Ella repeated the action words to herself, realizing now that others possessed this ability.

"Great," said the llama, "let's keep it going."

"Cool, I can go next," said the painted dog calmly. Then added, "unless you want to go instead." She was directing the question to Ella who didn't move an inch, so the dog continued. "Hi, I'm EE-go-lee-deh, but all my close friends call me Golee." She was long and lean with black fur and small white and yellow patches. "I guess three things about me would be that I am loyal, very overbearing and I wish to jump behind and support the group."

"Overbearing," said Chi, stepping into the circle and locking arms with the painted dog. "That's your untruth, isn't it?" Golee grinned and nodded, happy to have made a friend.

"Impressive," said Leader Llama, turning in Ella's direction. "Ella, will you wow us next?"

"Actually," the rodent interjected. "I was the fourth one to arrive at camp therefore it is more accurate that I should go next."

"By all means," said Leader Llama, yielding to her request. Ella was relieved to go last. She was busy mulling over the various ways each camper planned to use their jump. This unknown action seemed to be a necessity for getting through camp life.

"My formal name is Nutria pronounced NOO-tree-uh. Not, NUT-ree-uh, which is a common mistake and very annoying so you can all just call me Tria," said the rodent.

"First, I am consistent. Second," she pushed her glasses up on her nose. "I am adventurous. And third, I am planning to jump in and get things done."

"Are you kidding me?" thought Ella, starting to freak out. "The nutria also has Jump?"

"I know, I know," Otera chirped energetically. "It's adventurous, right? You're not adventurous. I could tell by the way you said it that you're not. There is no way in the world that you can be adventurous."

"Affirmative," Tria interjected, flashing an orange smile. "And finally," said the instructor as all eyes turned up to Ella.

"Well, um…" Ella hesitated, wishing she had thought about what to say before it was her turn. "I am Ella and I'm…" she could feel her tail stiffen as she searched for something, anything to say. "I'm a stay-putter," she blurted out.

"Interesting," said the llama, "what else?" Ella was thinking fast. "I'm afraid of bees," she revealed. "And …uhm I guess," everyone was watching intently. "I plan to jump up!"

"I got this," said Chi. "It's the bee fear. I mean you are ginormous. There's no way you are afraid of an itty-bitty bee."

Ella felt her neck grow warm as she assured Chi that her bee fear was very real.

"Alright, alright," Otera cheered. "Your untruth is the stay-putter thingy." She shrugged her shoulders, "Whatever that is."

Ella shook her large head. "No," she said. "That one is true too."

"But that only leaves," Tria deducted. "Do you mean that you don't plan to jump up?"

"Correct," replied Ella, feeling a flush creep across her face. "I don't have jump. At least I don't think I do." She said the last part mostly to herself.

"You poor thing," Golee said sympathetically. Everyone else remained speechless. The awkward silence was disrupted by a high-pitched scream from the llama.

"The morning is getting away from us," she announced. "Follow me!" And with that, she trotted off through the forest.

Pobody's Nerfect

Trailing behind the others, Ella remembered her mother's promise that she would have all that she needed in her trunk. She wished that she had followed Tria's lead and carried her pack instead of leaving it behind. "No worries," she consoled herself, "I will find jump in my trunk as soon as I get a chance to look for it." She reached the clearing just in time to see the llama ascending a large flat rock.

"This initiative," the leader bleated, clearly in her comfort zone, "is called the trust fall. Now, who will be the team leader for this activity?" She locked eyes on each of them, but every participant was looking at the cheetah, who appeared uncomfortable under the weighted stares.

"We can't always expect Chi to volunteer first," the llama intervened with a quick wink. Ella perceived a sense of relief on the young cheetah's face.

Then to everyone's surprise Golee jumped behind the llama. "I love doing this kind of thing," she said, grinning down at the motley crew.

The llama instructed those standing below. "Face one another in parallel lines, shoulder to shoulder, locking arms with the camper across from you. Then, on the count of three, Golee will land in our awaiting arms."

"Easy peasy," Golee hooted and without hesitation fell backward.

Otera and Tria took their turns, but Chi decided to sit this one out. Ella declined too, citing her inability to jump behind the others.

"Excellent job, everyone," their leader encouraged. "You have just learned a valuable Camp Get A Life lesson. Opportunities do not wait around. They come, and they go, and you must decide whether you wish to use your talents to lead, take part, or refuse to participate. There is no right or wrong answer. It's simply your own life experience. However, I do ask that you be conscious of the fact that inaction is still an action." She stood there blinking her lovely lashes, making eye contact with each camper before saying, "Now, for our next activity, all you have to do is look up."

Ella slowly tilted her head back as if expecting fire to fall from the sky. Overhead was a labyrinth of ropes, catwalks, and swings in the branches of the trees.

"The goal," said Leader Llama looking up at the ropes course, "is to participate in your best way."

"Awesome sauce!" Otera yelled, ignoring further instruction as she led the way by jumping out and catching the nearest branch.

"Cool," Golee said, feeling the excitement.

"Race you," challenged Chi.

Tria stood still and so did Ella. "You know, nutrias are bottom-heavy and therefore not very good climbers," she said to Ella, who was not sure if she was bragging or complaining.

"I had no idea," Ella replied.

"I did," Leader Llama broke into the conversation teeth first. "That is why I asked the logistics team to provide a sit-in harness. You see, Tria, after we secure it to a belay rope, we can hoist you up into the course."

"No, thank you." Tria cut her off. "Analytically thinking it doesn't seem like a perfect plan." Then added, "Nutrias are bottom heavy you know."

Ella, averting her eyes from the llama, reminded her of the fact that she could not jump out, and as everyone expected, Otera completed the course first, followed by Chi and Golee.

Bouncing on all fours, Leader Llama announced that next would be something everyone could participate in since it was also the way to the river. "Through orienteering and bushwhacking, we need someone to lead us to the whitewater initiative. How about you, Golee? Which way should we go?"

Golee, who so far had been relaxed, started fidgeting with one of her charm bracelets. "I'll pass that question to Chi" she replied, coolly twisting her mood ring.

"Good choice!" The cheetah quickly accepted before choosing a direction and jumping ahead, ordering the rest to follow.

Golee and Leader Llama took off behind her and Tria, after refer-ring to her own mental compass, followed suit. Ella, embarrassed by her inability to jump ahead, trudged along after them.

Otera, a bit exhausted from the ropes course, walked along with Ella and was happy to provide endless conversation.

Ella and Otera arrived at the river just in time to see Tria jump in behind a quickly built but perfectly crafted raft that carried Chi, Golee, and Leader Llama away from the bank.

The llama communicated to them through her megaphone, "We will meet you down river!" She waved animatedly as Tria led them through the river's currents.

Watching everyone pull away without her, Otera sighed and turned. She didn't feel like swimming much anymore and con-tinued walking alongside the river. Ella also passed, knowing she couldn't have jumped in even if she had wanted to.

The first thing that Ella spotted when they arrived at the campsite was the mound of personal items that the logistics crew had delivered, along with meal prep supplies and other necessities. Thank goodness, Ella thought, eyeballing her trunk in the middle of the bundle. She could not wait to look through it and find her much-needed jump.

It seemed as if time stood still as food was prepared, meals eaten, and the camp cleaned spotless. Finally, Leader Llama hud-dled everyone in to discuss the last challenge of the day.

Ella could hardly concentrate, sneaking glances at her trunk

every few seconds. "Come on," she thought, "let's get going."

"This solo portion allows for space to reflect on your life choices up until this very moment," their leader began. "I suggest that we practice complete silence as we head to our assigned areas. One by one, you will be dropped off at your solo sites. I understand that for some of you, solitary living is extremely rare. Please recognize that this solitude is meant to be a time of reflection, mindfulness, and maturity development."

Looking at them, the llama felt a lightness in her chest. Every group uniquely touched her heart and this one was no exception, but she was concerned about Ella. Finding furaha in life can be difficult when you are obsessed with how others are obtaining theirs.

A smile crossed her face. She still had faith in a Camp Get A Life transformation. After all, she was not just a coach. She had undergone the conversion firsthand. Like Ella, she had once attended camp GAL with her confidence rattled. But the experience of going outbound, away from her flock, had allowed her the time she needed to stop seeing herself as a carbon copy, always trying to imitate others. It did not take long for her to discover that through her talents of packing, forging, and her ability to coexist well with others her furaha was in leading expeditions and group facilitation therapy.

"Are we going to stand out here all night?" Asked an impatient Chi, jerking the llama back to the present.

So Low

Tria was dropped off first. Leader Llama thought she would enjoy finding a space near the edge of the riverbank. After her site was pointed out, Tria offered a salute, pushed up her glasses, and marched away.

Next was Otera, who struggled with the desire to say something motivating but instead gave a thumbs-up before running off to burrow in for the night.

Third was Chi, who promptly spotted a large shady tree, raised her index finger signaling "number one" stretched out her long muscular tail, and took off.

Golee, like Ella, was used to sleeping surrounded by her family. After glancing up at Ella sympathetically, Golee shared the peace sign and then walked away with her knap-sack slung over her shoulder.

Now, it was just Ella. As they walked along in silence, the coarse grass grew taller. Ella, fixating on finding jump in her trunk, could hardly wait to reach her drop-off destination.

Approaching Ella's solo site, Leader Llama resolved to discuss the elephant in the room. "Ella," she snorted and spat nervously, "we need to talk."

"What about your silence rule?" Ella asked.

The llama's expression softened. "Some rules are meant to be broken," she replied. Having Ella's attention, she continued, "I am aware that you have waited all day to unpack your trunk and find your jump."

Ella responded with a slow and foreboding "uuh-huuuh."

At that moment Leader Llama ripped off the Band-Aid. "I'm going to save you some trouble, Ella. You won't find jump in your trunk."

"What? Why are you saying that?"

"How could you know what I will or will not find in MY trunk?"

"I know that you won't find jump simply because," the llama took an exasperated breath, "elephants – can't - jump." She hesitated to make sure her words had sunk in.

"But… why?" Ella was shaking her head slowly in disbelief. Her dreams of jumping had crashed all around her.

"Well, it's an old story but as I understand it, jump was a gift given to all the animals for self-defense against predators. Being the largest land mammal and without a one-on-one predator, the elephant never needed this skill. Therefore," she offered an apologetic tooth-filled smile, "you don't have jump."

"But I need jump." Ella whined. "I must have it to survive Camp Get A Life."

"You may want it," the llama said, "but you don't need it."

"Of course, I do." Ella waved off the llama's attempt at

consolation. "The others have it and they use it to lead them to fu-raha. You were there! You saw it! Chi jumps ahead to be decisive. Golee jumps behind to be supportive. Otera jumps out to motivate, and Tria jumps in to get things done!"

The leader nodded her head. "Yes, yes," she acknowledged, "They all use their gift of jump in different ways to lead them and others to furaha. But," she paused waiting for Ella to stop swaying, "did you notice that Chi has a fear of losing control? That Tria is highly analytical? Golee is indecisive, and Otera fears being left out?"

"No," Ella said, starting to calm down. She hadn't paid attention to those things. She had been too busy fixating on their strengths and fretting over her lack of jump.

"Ella," the Llama said, "everyone has strengths and weak-nesses, and no animal is the whole package. The solution is to stop looking outward and start looking inward to discover your own furaha."

Ella responded with a confession. "But I'm afraid to try without jump."

"I get that," the llama said. "Camp Life can be a scary place. But there is a trick for when you feel stuck and afraid. Just ask yourself, can I do it anyway?" With that, she galloped off, dis-appearing into the savanna grass.

Ella cast a wistful glance in the direction where Leader Llama had skirted off before sighing and heading toward the place

selected for her. She was happy to see it was filled with her fa-
vorite vegetation. Sensing water was nearby she quickly freed the
belt from her waistline, allowing her bundle to drop to the ground.
After all, she shrugged her shoulders; it was useless to her now.

Ella settled under a clump of Acacia trees. Pulling out
her tarp, she hung it over a thick, high branch and used her trunk
fingers to tie it down securely before walking a short distance.
Locating the perfect spot, she pressed her foot firmly to the ground.
Using her trunk and legs, she created a small well, drank her fill,
and let the fresh water blanket her back before storing some for
later.

"You don't have jump in your trunk," she spoke harshly to
her reflection, staring back at her in the water.

To her surprise, her reflection looked more like her mother
than herself, and if what the llama had said was true, her mother,
the admired matriarch, did not possess jump either.

"That's ridiculous," Ella said to herself, stirring up the mud
from the bottom of the well. Queen Malika lacked nothing, and
hadn't she promised Ella that she would have everything she needed in her trunk?

"That's it!" Ella's heart sped up with a sudden burst of
clarity. "Whatever I need must still be in my trunk." Splashing mud
everywhere, Ella rushed back to the campsite with renewed ener-
gy to look through her belongings. She grabbed her bag and rifled
excitedly through it, pulling out every possession before raising her

eyes in disappointment. "Hold on," she said softly. "What is this?" Sewn into the lining at the very bottom of her bag, was something. Ripping the fabric, she took out a small, worn, leather-bound book. Turning it over, she read the title: *The Book of Courage*.

Ella recognized the book as belonging to her mother. On several occasions, she had seen her eagerly viewing its contents by the light of dawn. But Ella had no idea this small treasure had been passed down from matriarch to matriarch for more years than she could imagine.

Carefully opening the book, her sensitive trunk fingers felt the crispness of the first sheet compared to the rest of the delicate pages, affirming that it had been recently added. Ella's heart skipped a beat as she concentrated on the written words:

JUMP – ELLA'S MANTRA

Awaken the Elephant

Ella half expected to see her mother walk out of the bush. She had never heard the word jump mentioned in her entire life before attending camp, and now it was written inside an old book placed at the bottom of her trunk as if it had been waiting for her to find it. What does it all mean? How did her mother know about jump, and what did it have to do with her mantra? "What was her mantra anyway?" She wondered.

Ella remembered replacing the old negative mantra. Or … did she ever actually replace it? The talk with her mom seemed like ages ago but her excellent memory recalled it. "Take courage, take heart, cheer up" she began. "And then, just unpack my power. Yes, that was it! Cheer up and just unpack my power." Brushing clean a piece of earth with her trunk, she picked up a stick and wrote out the words of her mantra:

Cheer Up And Just Unpack My Power

Standing there as if in a trance she examined the words. Eyebrows furrowing then releasing, Ella dissected each letter bit by bit, gazing intently and with total focus. With tight lips and inward-looking eyes, she methodically underlined the first letters of the last four words.

JUST **U**NPACK **M**Y **P**OWER. She had found her **JUMP**.

Ella had so many questions, and every instinct told her the answers would be found in this little book. As a slight mist began falling, Ella ducked under her tarp and, grabbing a mouthful of

Acacia bark, snuggled up close to the tree. With a backdrop of buzzing cicadas, she began to read.

The book was filled with elephant history, elephant facts, elephant stories, elephant parables, and countless proverbs, mostly about elephants. Some of the proverbs were familiar, such as, 'No elephant complains about the weight of its trunk.' Others were puzzling, such as, 'When elephants fight, it is the grass that suffers. Ella felt invincible reading: Even if the elephant is thin, he is still the lord of the Jungle, but was humbled when reminded that the great jungle is stronger than the elephant. She especially enjoyed the parable "The Blind Men and the Indian Elephant," a simple story about a group of blind men who had never seen an elephant before. Yet each believed they understood all there was to know about elephants after only touching one part of it.

This story helped Ella see more clearly how different perspectives come from having received different information and that one should never judge the whole after only seeing a part.

She was grateful to learn from the book that her body was able to fight off cancer, and that elephants are among the few creatures who can communicate using low-pitched sounds called infrasound, which can cut through dense forests, across savannas, and even pass through mountains. Seeing in print that elephants need to eat three hundred pounds of food a day was not that surprising to Ella, but it still felt good to be validated. Fond memories rushed in while reading about how elephants show sensitivity to one another with calming gestures of physical contact. She was fascinated to find that in African folklore, elephants are revered as deities and symbols of both strength and wisdom.

But what inspired Ella the most was learning about the elephant trunk, which is a fusion of the upper lip and nose and in dexterity has no comparison in the animal kingdom. She had taken this unique gift for granted, never considering its tremendous capabilities.

An elephant's trunk is nature's multi-tool, she read eagerly. It has over 40,000 muscles and is used for breathing, smelling, drinking, and communicating. Being versatile, it can uproot trees one minute and then pluck a single leaf the next. It also has the sharpest sense of smell in the world, helping to locate water miles away, find food, identify family members, and assist with finding a perfect mate using chemical receptors. Its trumpeting can be heard for several miles, and by applying suction and inhaling air through the trunk, elephants can pick up food and other items above and beneath the water, thanks to their specialized respiratory system.

Ella also read that by contracting her nose muscles, she could carry six quarts of water for both cooling and drinking. "Interesting," she said, taking a drink from the store of water that she had gathered earlier, "my nose is like a trunk."

She gasped with sudden enlightenment: "My nose is like - a trunk?" And, with a grin that could not be contained, she dropped to her knees and affirmed excitedly: "And I have everything I need to be successful in my trunk!"

Let not what you cannot do tear
you from what you can do.

African Proverb

All through the night, Ella read page after page, growing more encouraged with each turn. Finally, with heavy eyelids, she wrapped the little book in her precious trunk. She replayed the last several months in her head with a new sense of self-awareness.

Painfully recalling how, after hearing the egret's comments, she allowed herself to become rigid and inflexible. Dominating and monopolizing conversations and feeling validated from the attention it brought her. She had dismissed others' input and made most decisions without collaborating with team members. Wincing, she recalled the times she responded negatively or was uninterested in the accomplishments of others. All for the sake of fooling herself into thinking that being an essential stay-putter could somehow replace being happy when proverbs say, "It is better to be happy than to be king."

Then yesterday! She moaned at the memory. Choosing not to join in and missing so many opportunities to make new friends, have fun, and share in life's challenges just because she did not have jump, when proverbs warn, "Let not what you cannot do tear you from what you can do." Worst of all, she believed a lie about her self-worth and in doing so had allowed it to overshadow her precious pursuit of furaha.

As Ella's confidence grew, so did her desire to improve herself and embrace challenges. Loudly addressing the grasslands, she proclaimed, "I love my upbeat personality and I take pleasure in being imaginative, inspiring others, and genuinely caring that they experience furaha in their lives. My contributions do add value, and if I ever get another opportunity at life," she bellowed, blared, and stomped her message with joy, "I won't waste it!"

Drained but happy, Ella slumped down against her tree, feeling content with a sense of euphoria. Lulled by the tranquilizing symphony of croaking frogs, she prayed, "I do hope to have another chance at life." Hearing her mother's voice reminding her that "hope never fails," she surrendered to sleep.

It is better to be happy than to be king.

African Proverb

The horned lark's delicate song nudged Ella awake an hour before the sun began its morning rise. With gratitude, she packed her bags under the cover of darkness, placing her book of courage in an accessible spot. "Your furaha is back," she spoke kindly to herself.

Strapping on her fanny pack and allowing her precious trunk to lead the way, she was soon back at the river's edge. Leader Llama was not surprised to see Ella show up first with her tail swinging and pep in her step, having heard her trumpeting during the night.

"Hello, Ella," she greeted her between chews of cud. "How are you feeling this morning?"

"Like an elephant," Ella responded. A smile brightened her face."Well, it's about time," Leader Llama confirmed.

The rest of the party began arriving. They were informed that the first initiative of the day would be to complete the whitewater river run. Tria had readied her raft and announced all aboard to her previous passengers.

Ella, noticing that Otera was turning to leave, exclaimed. "Proverbs say, if you want to go fast, go alone, but if you want to go far, go together. I will pull everyone if Tria steers."

Loving the idea, Tria, Golee, and Chi jumped aboard along with a perky Otera who was happy to be included.

Rising early makes the
road short.

African Proverb

Ella swam submerged in the deep water. She used her built-in snorkel for breathing and maneuvering the group through the high-volume river with its fast currents and crashing waves, before reaching a tranquil pool to the sound of cheers and whoops.

Once on land, it was time to navigate back to the ropes course.

Golee wavered, waiting to follow someone else's lead.

"You know Golee," Ella spoke with empathy while raising her trunk into the air, sniffing the wind to detect scents carried on the breeze. "Proverbs say, to get lost is to learn the way."

"Hey, that's deep," Golee said. "I think we should try this direction and see who can pick up our tracks from yesterday." She bounded off, the others following.

They all quickly traversed through the tall grass and found themselves back at the ropes course which looked just as intimidating to Tria as it did the first time.

"Hmm, I wonder," Ella said to no one in particular while watching the others begin their ascents.

"Yes," said Tria inquisitively, "you were saying?"

"Oh, I was just thinking that instead of hoisting oneself up, one could find a tree to use to make a ramp, then one could at least," she glanced quickly at Tria, "take part in the course."

Eyeing the perfect tree, Tria noted, "Well, it's not ideal."
"No, I agree it's not," Ella replied. "But I bet we could have some fun trying it.

If you want to go fast, go alone,
but if you want to go far,
go together.

African Proverb

To get lost is to learn the way.

African Proverb

Besides, as the proverb says, the hands that make a mistake belong to those who work."

"That's factual," the Nutria answered. "Let's go for it!"

Ella leaned her head against the selected tree. She wrapped her trunk around it with a strong grip and then dug her tusks into the bark. Pushing and pulling with her trunk she leaned the tree into the obstacle course and Tria walked up the incline to join the fun.

After experiencing the challenges of the ropes course, it was time for the last activity of the day. The final trust fall.

Ella, assuming Chi planned to pass on this activity, declared suddenly. "I'll do it!"

"You?" Chi asked. "You still can't jump," she reminded Ella bluntly.

"You're right," Ella smiled, acknowledging the criticism. "But she who does not know one thing knows another, and proverbs also say, if you fear something, you give it power over you."

After hearing this ancient truth, Chi set her jaw and with one extraordinary leap reached the top of the rock, prompting everyone below to scurry into their spotting positions before she jumped ahead.

The hands that make a mistake belong to those who work.

African Proverb

Otera jumped out after her. Golee jumped behind Otera and Tria jumped in next.

Once again, all eyes were on Ella as she gradually climbed to the top of the rock. She was thinking of the herd back home and all the opportunities it offered her to experience true furaha through mentoring, foraging, herd protection, maintaining forest health, travel, community engagement, and providing care and development. With her new mindset, the possibilities now seemed endless, and she was anxious to return and celebrate her siblings' accomplishments, recognizing now that she, too, had all she need-ed to obtain furaha for herself.

Reaching the top of the rock, Ella looked down at the friendly faces that before had seemed strange and aloof. She thought about how far she had come in the last two days and determined never to be a stay-putter again. Ella was convinced that she could protect her furaha as long as she built on her talents, developed her abilities, embraced her gifts, and sharpened her skills, remaining mindful of the valuable lessons she acquired along the way. Self-assured that just because you don't have one thing doesn't mean you don't have no-thing.

And she would forever carry within her the leadership examples of her wonderful new friends:

If you fear something, you give it
power over you.

African Proverb

Chi's determination, confidence, and productiveness; Golee's calmness, thoughtfulness, and adaptability; Otera's optimism, risk-taking, and motivation; and Tria's self-discipline, focus, and persistence.

Ella now realized that none of them were perfect, but they each were leaders just the same.

"Jump, Ella!" her friends cheered her on.

At peace with the fact that she did not have jump, Ella trusted that her mantra would never fail her as she rehearsed the words in her head. "When I feel stuck, I will cheer up, and Just Unpack My Power." Then, smiling confidently, she said aloud: "I'll JUMP!"

And that... is exactly what she did.

Just because you don't have
one thing doesn't mean you
don't have no-thing.

No Jump in my Trunk

Author's Note - The Hidden Narrative of No Jump in My Trunk

In the hustle and bustle of everyday life, it's easy to lose sight of who you truly are. *No Jump in My Trunk* seeks to illuminate the path to self-awareness, empowering you to reconnect with your authentic self and unpack your power.

Allow me to share with you the motivation that influenced the story of *No Jump in My Trunk* and to provide a fuller understanding of the truth that it uncovers.

I started writing this little story of courage in the middle of a worldwide pandemic when the work that we did and the activities that we enjoyed were split into two categories: essential and non-essential.

The professional life that I knew and enjoyed was placed in the latter, and when the feelings of not having what it took to be essential began to emerge, I now possessed the mental tools to fight back.

But that was not always so.

No Jump in My Trunk mirrors my voyage to taking courage. This fable illustrates how I stopped feeling afraid and stuck and started playing the cards life had dealt me. Equipped in the full armor of God, I learned how to silence the untruths and utilize my talents and gifts to find true joy and happiness.

This parallel narrative takes place in the African Savannah, where a young elephant must succeed at finding happiness without possessing "jump," a metaphor for specific talents and attributes that you do not possess but believe you must have to be successful in life.

Jump can be innate or inborn such as physical attractiveness, athleticism, musical talent, artistic aptitude, leadership qualities, spatial awareness, linguistic abilities, creativity, height, body type, health, resilience, mathematical capacity, and cognitive thinking.

Jump can also be an entitlement such as inheritance, wealth, social class, culture, family reputation, citizenship, genetic health, parental support, access to education, an entrepreneurial spirit, exposure to arts, travel, and family influence and connections.

Realizing she can't jump, the protagonist accepts the falsehood that her happiness hinges on having jump. This combination of "no jump-need jump" creates a closed mindset that harbors resistance to new ideas and perspectives, leading her to minimize or disregard her actual skills.

Through numerous speaking engagements with diverse audiences, I have learned that we all encounter not having Jump at some point in our personal and professional lives. I can also speak from experience that genuine self-reflection, leveraged with your personal strengths will guide you towards forging, competing, and contributing your way to a fulfilling life.

Stirred Not Shaken

At the age of 21 on a 7-day outdoor educational challenge, 50 feet high in a tree, deep in the Nantahala National Forest, I realized that I didn't have Jump. Unable to retrace my steps and unwilling to move forward I simply gave up and sat down.

My instructor, seated comfortably on the ground, yelled up to ask what was wrong.

I anxiously replied that I was afraid, but there was more to it. I wasn't just afraid at that time; I had been afraid for the last five years. Having made a major life choice in my late teens, I found myself fearful of failure, my confidence shaken by its impact.

No Jump met me as I approached the high balance beam of the ropes course. The teammate in front of me appeared to easily walk across the beam by steadying himself with an overhead branch and after witnessing his display of reach, my five-foot frame felt helpless to make it across. "You need to be taller to make your way through this ropes course" was the lie playing in my head, and being tall was the Jump that I lacked in that moment.

"I know you're afraid," the facilitator picked up the conversation from below, then asked, "but, can you do it anyway?"

Inspired by her words, I stood on my feet, approaching

the challenge with everything that was in me. To my surprise, out came my talent of balance, which had developed and improved through years of ballet classes. Crossing the beam with ease, I wasn't just doing it anyway. I was doing it my way.

Then, in my early 30s, the company that I worked for moved to a new city and I learned of a job opportunity with a small brokerage firm close to home. Jump was a mathematical ability and I had always found math challenging.

The untruth associated with this lack of Jump was that I needed to excel in math to succeed in the financial world. Finding the courage to promote the gifts that I had, I discovered that my skills in reading comprehension, customer service, and enthusiasm for learning proved me well for 17 wonderful years with the firm.

Later, in my 40s, Jump was health related. Alopecia is a genetic, autoimmune disorder that affects 2% of the population where the immune system mistakenly attacks the hair follicles, causing partial or total hair loss. After 20 years of fighting this condition with medication, I stopped taking the steroids and not long after, my immune system completed its attack.

This time Jump was a beautiful head of hair, and the falsehood was that I needed my hair to face the world each day. Fighting the desire to retreat self-consciously, instead, I launched *Cheer up and Live!* a motivational company that has guided hundreds of clients to take courage and move.

Approaching my mid-50s, with years of practicing introspection, I realized that Jump was being considered essential. This time I was not afraid nor was I shaken, and with a mindset focused on personal development and self-improvement, I stirred up my gifts and started on a hero's journey of writing a story of personal transformation.

No Jump in My Trunk explores overcoming internalized falsehoods maintained due to fear or insecurity, teaching valuable lessons about humility, acceptance of one's limitations, and the recognition that everyone possesses their own unique strengths and weaknesses, which are essential to their personal growth and self-acceptance.

You will uncover how the grip of imposter syndrome loosens by recognizing and challenging negative thoughts, replacing them with more truthful and affirming beliefs.

You will also discover the importance of supportive communities and mentors while observing how to effectively use soft skills when working with different personalities and leadership types to promote collaboration and understanding.

And finally, you'll come to appreciate the transformative power of self-awareness and its profound influence on how we perceive ourselves and others.

THE IMPACT OF SELF-AWARENESS

Positive self-awareness means having a clear and realistic understanding of your strengths, weaknesses and emotions, and involves recognizing what you can achieve with your current abilities and resources.

It is an essential skill in numerous professions, boosting personal effectiveness, strengthening interpersonal relationships, and increasing overall job satisfaction.

Self-awareness helps you understand your reactions to challenges, stresses, and emotional triggers and is a key component of emotional intelligence.

By coupling the soft skill of self-awareness with a growth mindset, you can make better decisions and set realistic goals, ultimately becoming more effective and adaptable in your career.

How Self-Awareness Transforms
Different Careers

Self-Aware Sales People realize their communication styles, enabling them to customize their approach to better connect with clients and future opportunities through personalized selling strategies that resonate more effectively with different groups of people.

Self-Aware Leaders and Managers improve decision-making, team management, and conflict resolution by understanding their own leadership style and impact on others. Facilitating better alignment with personal values and organizational objectives.

Self-Aware Customer Service Representatives better manage stress and maintain a positive attitude when dealing with challenging situations, leading to better customer interactions.

Self-Aware Financial Advisors understand their strengths and weaknesses, allowing them to communicate more effectively, build trust with clients, and tailor their approach to meet each client's unique needs, making more objective, rational decisions.

Self-Aware Human Resource Professionals better understand their biases and preferences, leading to more objective and effective hiring practices. Healthy self-awareness also enhances the ability to manage conflicts and understand employee needs.

Self-Aware Athletes can identify when they are feeling stressed and employ strategies to calm or motivate themselves. It also allows them to focus on improving specific areas while leveraging their strengths, leading to enhanced overall performance.

Self-Aware Nonprofit Team Members appreciate their talents and passions, enabling them to align their personal goals with the organization's mission. Resulting in greater dedication, commitment and increased engagement.

Self-Aware Hospitality Associates impact the quality of service and guest satisfaction. Understanding their emotions, hospitality professionals can remain calm, patient, and positive in challenging situations, leading to better service, communication, and effective conflict resolution.

Self-Aware Educators and Trainers are better equipped to understand their teaching style, strengths, and areas for improvement. This awareness allows them to adapt their methods to suit different learning styles, making their instruction more effective and inclusive.

Self-Aware Health Care Professionals enhance communication, leading to better patient interactions. Understanding their biases, strengths, and limitations leads to more empathetic and patient-centered care.

Self-Aware Property Managers can better understand their communication style and its impact on tenants and colleagues, leading to clearer, more effective interactions. Recognizing personal strengths and limitations allows property managers to seek help or delegate tasks, improving problem- solving efficiency.

Self-Aware College and Graduate Students communicate effectively with peers, professors, and mentors by understanding their own triggers, emotions, and reactions. They also learn from their failure and setbacks, leading to personal growth and resilience.

Self-Aware Information Technologists are more likely to engage in projects that align with their values contributing to the greater good. They are also better equipped to make ethical decisions, designing more empathetic and inclusive technologies.

Self-Aware Creative Professionals recognize their unique talents, which allows them to produce original and innovative work. They also embrace constructive feedback, realize areas for improvement and actively seek new techniques, skills, or knowledge to expand their creative range.

In summary, practicing self-awareness allows us to embrace and value our abilities and strengths while fostering a true appreciation for the skills of those around us. This change in outlook promotes a more positive and supportive atmosphere to flourish and work together effectively.

People are more uplifted, energetic, and at peace when they recognize their assets and are encouraged to work with their skills. This allows them to utilize their strengths, feel competent, and experience a sense of achievement, enjoying greater job satisfaction and engagement.

Whether seeking personal growth, professional success, or a renewed sense of purpose, *No Jump in My Trunk* shares motivating aphorisms and actions to empower you on your journey toward fulfillment and success.

ACKNOWLEDGMENTS

I would like to express my heartfelt gratitude to the following individuals who supported me throughout the journey of writing this book:

My Husband: When I couldn't see my way, you were there shining a light.

My Family: Your belief in me kept me motivated during challenging times.

Friends and Reviewers: Thank you for your support and encouragement. Your feedback was instrumental in shaping this work.

A special thank you to Ben Precup for his creativity and skill in designing the cover of this book.

 The proverbs used in this book reflect the wisdom and traditions of various African communities and I acknowledge and honor the contributions of these cultural expressions to the content of my work.

Dweck,Carol S. Mindset: The New Psychology of Success. Random House 2006

John Trent, whose work on personality models using animals, inspired aspects of this fable.

The ancient Greek physician Hippocrates and the Roman physician Galen for their foundational work in developing the theory of the four temperaments—sanguine, choleric, melancholic, and phlegmatic.

I want to convey the use of Open AI's ChatGPT, which provided detailed information on the role of self-awareness in various professions that was instrumental in shaping that section of the book. The illustrations were created with the assistance of Bing Image Creator, based on my creative direction. I acknowledge the role of the tool in helping bring my visual concepts to life.

My deep appreciation goes to Outward Bound, whose outdoor challenge in 1989 left a lasting impression on me. That experience helped shape my understanding of perseverance, teamwork, and personal growth, all of which are reflected in the fable within this book.

INTERACTIVE ACTIVITIES FOR SELF-AWARENESS, TEAM BUILDING, AND INCLUSION

To complement the themes in No Jump in my Trunk, I have designed a series of engaging and interactive activities aimed at enhancing a growth mindset, fostering team collaboration, and promoting positive self-awareness. These activities are ideal for college and university programs, as well as all teams, community groups, and professional organizations looking to foster self-awareness, teamwork and personal growth. Download printable worksheets and guides at *cheerupandlive.com*

Temperament Showdown A fun, fast-paced game that introduces participants to the power of personality types through interactive hand signals. This activity helps participants understand and appreciate diverse temperaments while engaging in a team challenge. Look for extra tips and bonus activities at *cheerupandlive.com*

Trust Net A team-building exercise where groups form a supportive "net" with their arms, encouraging trust and collaboration as they catch a falling team member. Perfect for strengthening bonds in a short amount of time. Find the detailed steps online at *cheerupandlive.com.*

Tightrope Tango Teams strive for balance while walking a rope on the ground facing obstacles that challenge their coordination. The game highlights the desire for perfection but reveals that true success lies in embracing support and flexibility rather than flawless execution. Head to *cheerupandlive.com* for more detail.

Quickfire Directions This fast-paced game forces participants to make split-second decisions as they respond to random direction prompts. Designed to challenge indecisiveness, it encourages quick action and trusting one's instincts, showing that sometimes the best choice is simply making one. For extra tips and bonus activities, visit *cheerupandlive.com*.

The Shrinking Circle Participants must work together to fit into an ever-shrinking space, forcing them to adapt and strategize quickly. As the space tightens, the game stirs feeling of exclusion, highlighting the anxiety of being left out while encouraging creative solutions and teamwork to ensure everyone remains included. Visit *cheerupandlive.com* for full instructions!

Stirring the Gift This reflective activity takes participants back to their childhood passions, helping them rediscover forgotten talents and interests. By reconnecting with their innate gifts, participants gain positive self-awareness, recognizing their strengths they've always had and how these gifts can enrich their lives today. Check out *cheerupandlive.com* to learn more.

To Learn More If you're looking to integrate these activities into your orientation programs or team building initiatives, please visit *cheerupandlive.com* for more information.

ABOUT THE AUTHOR

Chrissie Dixon is a first-time author and lifelong encourager, known for her humorous, interactive, faith-filled speaking and training sessions.

Raised in a small town in North Carolina, Chrissie grew up surrounded by the love and support of her family, church, and community.

Her unique, cheerful approach, blended with personal insights and practical strategies, has touched many lives, empowering people to overcome fear and acknowledge and appreciate their inherited value.

Her mission is to ignite a spark of hope and determination in everyone she meets, believing that with the right mindset and tools, anyone can achieve their goals and live a fulfilling life.

When Chrissie is not writing or speaking, she enjoys riding on the motorcycle with her husband, John, on the Blue Ridge Parkway and spending time with her large and loving family.

www.ingramcontent.com/pod-product-compliance
Lightning Source LLC
Chambersburg PA
CBHW071238090426
42736CB00014B/3137